SAILING THE STORM OF LOGIC

Dear Beverley

Create your own

Storm. my friend.

Sailing the Storm of Logic

Brian (Watt) Bakeberg

Print Edition
First Edition
Copyright © Brian (Watt) Bakeberg
ISBN: 978-1-916544-27-7

Publishing Information

Design & publishing services
provided by JM Agency

www.jm.agency
Kerry, Ireland

A Journey Towards Personal Fulfilment

SAILING THE STORM OF LOGIC

Challenging the Boundaries of Logic

BRIAN BAKEBERG

A true maverick, Brian continually pushes boundaries and challenges conventional thinking. The book invites readers to be inspired by his extraordinary journey, offering valuable lessons on embracing logic, defying conventions and unleashing your power within; your ability to achieve genuine greatness.

This book provides the reader with a rare insight into the author's journey to personal fulfilment. It Is full of practical gems, insights and behaviours to assist all those people who seek personal fulfilment.

*The logic concept, combined with the author's experiences, makes this book different. He creates simple but not simplistic models e.g. **launch**, **storm**, **landing**, which are easy to remember and implement.*

This book is well written and illustrated with lots of practical examples – ideal for those in pursuit of personal fulfilment. As the author says, "Make it Fun and Get it Done".

– Shay McConnon
Author, Global Keynote Speaker and Psychologist

Contents

Foreword

In this captivating memoir, prepare to embark on a profound journey through the relentless storm with my logic. You will read the transformative experiences that shaped my destiny and discover the power of resilience and determination in logic.

From the exhilarating débuts of my many entrepreneurial pursuits, to the challenges, failures and victories that followed, I have navigated the turbulent waters of business with unwavering determination. Through it all, I unravelled the true essence of greatness and redefined my unique place in the world.

Join me on this introspective voyage as I delve deep into the storm that both consumed and shaped me. As you turn each page, you will read stories of raw honesty and vulnerability which is the main foundation of my journey. Together, we will explore the inner workings of my logic, witnessing the battles lost, the lessons learned, and, ultimately, the triumphs achieved.

This is not just a memoir; it is a testament to the invincible human spirit within us all.

It serves as a guiding light for those who have faced their own storms, reminding us that within every challenge lies an opportunity for growth and transformation.

Whether you are an aspiring entrepreneur seeking inspiration, a dreamer in pursuit of greatness or simply someone navigating the storms of life, this memoir will resonate with you on a profound level. Prepare to be moved, inspired and empowered as you sail alongside me on this extraordinary journey.

So, grab an oar, strap on your life vest, and get ready to embark on an unforgettable voyage. Together, we will navigate the storm of logic and uncover the true power that lies within each and every one of us.

Introduction

Living in a world filled with rules and expectations, I have always felt a deep sense of discomfort with the conventional path that society laid out before me. In this book, I share my journey of challenging the fabric of logic itself and embracing personal fulfilment.

So as a foundation for my writing, I need to explain where the motivation comes from.

My wife Orla is a phenomenal author and natural light photographer and reminds me that I am her number one biggest supporter. Check her out (www.orlaphotography.ie)

Orla sees *the picture in the picture*.

Which resonates with me seeing *the logic in the logic*.

We have had many discussions over the years about her photos and how she manages to capture the essence of the picture.

When we moved to Geesala in the West of Ireland in 2022, my mind started to steer me to writing this book.

Geesala is a small rural village with the heart of a giant. The people in this area are so welcoming, and I really resonated with the culture and ambiance of the village. Alongside the people in the community, it consists of two pubs, a stunning hotel, community centre, stunning beaches and a diverse landscape. Don't all come running but put it on your list of places you need to spend a few days at, if you are ever transversing the beautiful Emerald Isle.

With all this beauty around us, I started showing a greater interest in the book that Orla was writing, *Life Threads*, and how she captured each picture in a story.

She told me I had to look at *the picture in the picture*. That's when I got it, which led me to realise that we must look at *the logic in the logic*.

So, that is when I started recapturing the logic in my logic and all that has passed during my life, which has brought me to believe there is a story to be told and shared.

During this time, I found my happy place from a business which was for sale called, 'An Even Better Place to Work.' My every being, my inner logic and all I have stood for most of my adult life, aligned perfectly with the ethos of this business. So, I bought it. I will share more of that story later.

Logic is defined as a proper or reasonable way of thinking about something. It should be considered socially acceptable, fair and sensible. But whose logic are we following? Do not let other people's logic determine your destiny. People who follow other logic remain mediocre. It is those who influence the logic that stand out. We were not brought into this world to be mediocre. Stand out and be brilliant.

My story has three steps – *The Launch, The Storm and The Landing*. *The Launch* is where it all began and the point of entry into my conscious mind. *The Storm* is the period of struggle and change within my life, calming my subconscious mind. *The Landing* is the point when I realised I had fulfilled my own greatness through my own logic. Being in control of your conscious and your subconscious mind is like seeing a lighthouse after the storm.

Success or failure, the shackles of struggle are removed.

The following chapters will guide you through some of these stormy waters.

ONE

Defying Societal Norms

I recently spent some time researching my genealogy, which was handed down to me by my late mother, whose maiden name was Alicia Mary Watt.

I had been shown the family tree numerous times but never really considered its significance. Some of her findings included my fifth great grandfather whose name was James Watt FRS, FRSE (19 January 1736 – 25 August 1819). He was a Scottish inventor, mechanical engineer and a chemist.

He was known for his significant improvements to Thomas Newcomen's 1712 steam engine, which resulted in the creation of the Watt steam engine in 1776. This invention played a fundamental role in driving the changes brought about by the Industrial Revolution, not only in Great Britain but globally.

My great grandfather's ability to focus his energy and logic on things he could influence, rather than those he could not, earned him the reputation of a great leader. Statues all over Britain are testament to him and he was even featured on the £50 note, up until recently.

As his great grandchild, I believe I have inherited his keen sense for change. Both he and I are engineers and we share a joint passion for championing logic change.

My great grandfather's pursuit of influencing logic was evident in his numerous inventions, such as the Watt steam engine, Watt's linkage, Watt's curve, separate condenser, centrifugal governor, horsepower, indicator diagram, letter copying press, sun and planet gear and many others. Through these innovations, he aimed to redefine established practices and shape the future by influencing the logic.

What set him apart was his ability to combine a theoretical knowledge of science with practical application, guided by his personal logic. His achievements went beyond being a great practical mechanic. My great grandfather's profound understanding of natural philosophy and chemistry, as demonstrated through his inventions, showcased his genius and his ability to influence the logic.

His contributions earned him the respect and admiration of his contemporaries during the Industrial Revolution. He was an esteemed member of the Lunar Society of Birmingham and a highly sought-after conversationalist and companion, always eager to expand his horizons. His legacy and logic continue to inspire generations of engineers and innovators around the world today. This drive and logic must be in the DNA!!

From an early age, I had a different vision of success to others. I believed that true power and uniqueness lay in the ability to shape one's own life, to create a reality that defied the limitations set by others. Not dissimilar to my great grandfather's own beliefs.

In this chapter, I explore the discomfort I felt with societal expectations and the unconventional path I chose to pursue.

From the moment I first became aware of the world around me, I knew deep within my being that success meant more than just conforming to societal expectations. It was about breaking free from the mould and forging my destiny. In this chapter, I delve into the profound sense of unease I experienced with the constraints imposed by society and the audacious path I boldly embarked upon. My elder brother had a picture in his office that stated, 'The mediocre are always at their best.' From the moment I saw that picture I knew I would never aim to be mediocre, average or ordinary. I knew the world had a special purpose for me if I wanted it, which I did.

I have always heard something different when people speak to me. I always hear what I want to hear and that is my interpretation of the logic.

I used to sit with my father and talk to him about what I wanted to do, and he would tell me exactly the way to do it, the exact steps I was to take. I would then go armed with his advice and knowledge and know exactly how it was to be done and do it differently. My father would see what I was doing and come to me and say, "Brian we discussed this, why are you not doing it like I explained?" My answer was simple, "Dad, you explained how it has always been done and how it is guaranteed to work but is that the best way to do it? If I make mistakes along the way I will always know where to step back from and what is coming, so my logic can adapt my strategy to get to the same result."

Sometimes this took longer and was more costly but sometimes my logic found a better and quicker way to get the same result. My continual use of this logic helped me to streamline my thought process and the mistakes became less and the journeys became quicker.

Hindsight, procedures, protocols and rules have one thing in common - it is constructed by few to control the outcome of energy of many. It is their logic, their experiences and the experiences of others who have gone before them that guide them.

It is not without failure that one learns, it is inevitably failure that teaches us. If we focus on failure, we will never see the opportunity it is showing us.

As a child, I yearned for something greater, something extraordinary that went beyond the ordinary milestones set by others. My English teacher told me I was un-educatable and would amount to nothing, and my late father used to tell me I had dreams of grandeur.

I was driven by a burning desire to wield true power and embrace my unique identity. It was this relentless pursuit of authenticity that led me to question the very foundations upon which society was built. The need to create wealth led me to external logic or the lack thereof.

The Launch is where it began; the point of entry in my subconscious mind and the power of the subconscious. The power it holds is an essential aspect of our psychological makeup. By exploring and understanding the subconscious, we can unlock its potential to positively influence our logic, emotions, thoughts and actions; leading to personal transformation and fulfilment. The subconscious mind is often associated with our deepest desires, fears and beliefs and it can greatly impact our self-perception, habits and overall well-being. By understanding and harnessing the power of the subconscious, we can work towards reprogramming negative thought patterns, overcoming limiting beliefs and achieving personal growth and success through subconscious logic. The subconscious mind has its own individual private logic that might be vastly different than the conscious mind's logic which is governed by external forces.

The Storm is the period in the middle when you need to fight for common ground within your life and the blood sweat and tears of it all. During this process, you will need to work out what you stand for, what your emotions are, what your thoughts are and be guided by your actions and your subconscious logic. If you genuinely want to be an adventurer and influence your logic, you will need to remember that you will often stand alone and people will want to steer you out of the storm. It is always easier to go around the storm, like people have done before you.

The Landing is the point when you realise you have fulfilled your own greatness by implementing your own logic. My wise young brother calls this life scars. I like to think of it more as being like physical scars, but life scars can serve as reminders of past pain and struggles. However, they can also be seen as a testament to your own resilience and strength in overcoming adversity. Life scars can shape your character, influence your logic, beliefs, behaviour and relationships.

In the pages that follow, you will witness the struggles, triumphs and revelations that propelled me towards a path less travelled. I invite you to embrace the courage it takes to break free from the shackles of conformity and embark on a journey of self-discovery and personal fulfilment.

My first hard lesson and probably the start of my journey must be the moment I realised my thought process was not the same and my subconscious needed to be exercised to create my own logic.

The Launch
My First Recollection of Logic

I had an uncle who visited us once when I was about five, a man who always had time for fun and games with us as children.

Somehow, we were talking about gambling and betting, and he said to me, "Brian my boy, I bet you I can jump higher than this house."

He had my attention. We walked outside, I looked at the roof and then I looked at my uncle. I did some quick five-year-old calculations and replied, "How much?"

He said, "Whatever is in your money box."

So, I said, "Ok, but if you can't, how much will you pay me?"

He said, "Double your money."

That was a good deal if I won but I wanted to see if I could get more, so I said, "No, 10 times my money."

He looked at the house, looked at me, and thought a bit, before saying , "Ok, I am pretty sure I can jump higher than the house."

Well, this shocked me. I knew already I had money in my money box, more than enough for an ice-cream soda and even a trip to the cinema, so this was a hard decision.

I studied the roof and then studied my uncle's height. He confirmed he would do it from a standing position and he would not touch the roof.

At that point, after exhausting all options, it was a no-brainer.

So, I said, "Yes, we have a deal."

He took a hop into the air and asked how high it was. I laughed and said about one foot; he had about 30 more to go in order to clear the top.

I could already see the big party happening with all my friends.

He smiled at me and spoke, "Are you sure it was one foot?" I confirmed it was one foot.

He then said to me, "That's it, now you make the house jump." This was where the logic started.

We did discuss this in detail but nonetheless, I handed my money box over and off he went.

Defying societal norms is just the beginning of an extraordinary tale that has challenged my perception of logic, success and inspiration, questioned the status quo and ignited a flame of rebellion within my soul.

So, take a deep breath, open your mind, and prepare to embark on a transformative adventure that will leave a permanent mark on your heart and mind.

All things are possible.

By the way, when I turned 21, my uncle gave me my money box back complete and untouched and included a full collector's set of the country's coins for that year. I had by then refined my listening and conversational skills, and logically analysing their statements, which is something I continue to do.

TWO

Navigating Storms & Battling Opposition

Throughout my life, I faced countless storms and battles. Society told me to conform and to accept the norms but I remained steadfast in my pursuit of personal fulfilment.

This chapter serves as a testament to the challenges I have faced and the unyielding resilience I have cultivated in the face of relentless opposition. Never being worried about things I could do nothing about.

In the journey of my life, I have encountered an abundance of storms and battles. Society, with its pressures to conform and embrace the norms, constantly tried to steer me off course. However, I stood firm in my unwavering pursuit of personal fulfilment. This chapter serves as a testament to the challenges I have faced and the unyielding resilience I have cultivated in the face of relentless opposition.

As I recount my experiences, I delve into the various obstacles that have assessed my resolve. From societal expectations that threatened to stifle my individuality, to the naysayers who doubted my dreams. I confronted a range of opposition that could have easily deterred me. But instead of succumbing to these external pressures, I chose to harness them as catalysts for growth.

Within these pages, I share the valuable lessons I have learned from navigating through the tempestuous storms of life. Each setback became an opportunity for self-reflection, enabling me to discover my true strengths and unravel the depths of my resilience. Through the battles I fought, I discovered the power of determination and the unwavering belief in my abilities and my logic.

This chapter not only explores the challenges I have encountered but also provides insights into the strategies I employed to overcome them. From developing a strong mindset, to seeking support from like-minded individuals, I reveal the logical techniques that have helped me weather the storms and emerge stronger.

With every adversity I faced, I refused to surrender to the pressures of conformity and instead embraced the path less sailed. I hope that by sharing my journey, readers will find inspiration and empowerment to navigate their storms, armed with the knowledge that resilience and determination can lead to extraordinary personal fulfilment.

The Storm is a period of struggle and change in my life whereas *The Landing* is the point when I realised I had fulfilled my own greatness through my own logic. Success or failure, the shackles were being removed. Only you can tell yourself when you can remove these shackles.

The Storm

Born in 1964 in Johannesburg, South Africa, I was educated at Discover Primary School. I played first-team cricket, participated in drama classes and I was also a library prefect.

Between the years of nine and thirteen, I learned ballroom and Latin American dancing and was the champion in South Africa in many of these categories.

I then moved to Florida Park High Senior School in 1983. Here, I was a school prefect, cross country captain, hockey captain, swimming team captain, cricket captain, athletics captain and part of the drama society. I loved my years at school and I can fondly remember waking up, running to the bus stop, handing them my bag and racing the school bus on foot, about four kilometres to school and being there before the bus arrived, where I would open the gates to the school and let everybody in.

After school, I did conscription, mandatory military service for two years, where I qualified as an instructor.

I became a vegetarian upon joining the army. I was quick to learn that their food was specially prepared and came out of the officer's dining room and kitchen.

Whereas all other food was generally mass-produced slop covered in gravy.

My first official job was in 1986 with Elida Gibbs, which was part of the Unilever Group of companies. I was employed as a merchandiser. I was quickly promoted to an assistant sales representative, and by October 1986 I was allocated the Northwestern Province as a country area manager. I embraced every moment, every day, but eventually I got bored, as targets and budgets were all too easy to achieve. I was young and searching for myself, testing my logic.

In December 1986, I resigned and turned to refrigeration and air conditioning engineering. My cousin was opening a small branch for the company he worked for and one Sunday after tennis he got a callout to a local supermarket to fix a huge fridge and I went with him. I loved it. The following Monday, I resigned from my job at Unilever and went with him to open the branch. He could not pay me at first, so I boarded and lodged with him.

I furthered my studies as a mechanical engineer focusing on refrigeration and air-conditioning. I did my practical internship with a Dutch-based company called Smeva Ltd. I was involved with many big commercial and industrial contracts during this time. I lived on a banana and avocado farm and survived on bananas and avocados as part of my staple diet.

In 1989, after qualifying, I relocated to Botswana to open my first business at the age of twenty five and remained self-employed after that.

My brother and father had opened a sales and distribution company in Botswana, called Kalahari Sales, in 1986, and were doing well. Believing I could do better, I set up my own company, to compete. It worked, as I could then represent some brands and they could represent the competitive brands.

This was my first business, United Marketing Pty Ltd.

It was a fast-moving consumer goods, sales and distribution agency. I represented large multinational food manufacturing companies. Things were not easy at first and money was scarce, but I kept going. I also got married to my first wife, which added some financial pressure; this did drive my inner being to achieve.

Around the same time, I also opened a business called Ref-Tec Botswana (Refrigeration Technology Botswana), my second business, in 1990, which included working for the Senn Foods Group, the biggest Independent Abattoir in Botswana under contract to Smeva Holland.

In 1991, I merged United Marketing with Kalahari Sales and worked alongside my brother and father where I once again became involved with Unilever as a distributor.

The reason for the merger was twofold –

1. To create a larger, stronger business.
2. To be able to focus on my other business interests.

I set up a cold room storage facility for Kalahari Sales for Van Den Bergh & Jurgens, part of the Unilever group specialising in margarine, before closing Ref-Tec Botswana down in 1993, when Smeva Holland pulled out of the African market. In 1992, I started a safety match business called Tau Match (which means 'Lion' in Setswana, Botswana's native language) with my partner Kgosiemang Molosiwa, and in 1993 we also started a candle factory called SuperLite Candles which worked well with my match factory.

In December 1993, I sold my share in Kalahari Sales and left, as I had a disagreement with my partners about my logic. Not everybody understands it, and, also, working with family is not always an easy road.

I have had this discussion with many people along my journey - fundamentally people do not wake up in the morning and go to work to annoy you, make mistakes or get into trouble; it is the exact opposite. If you do not take the time to ensure that people who work for you and who are around you, are not made to feel special, how can you expect any respect from anybody? People generally do the best they can. Perhaps a simple hand up, a compassionate word or taking the time to care, is all that is needed to turn something good into something great.

After leaving Kalahari Sales, I remember sitting in my match factory with a door placed on two drums being used as my desk to work from. I was contemplating how I was going to make money and support my family as I had just found out that I was going to be a father.

This was both a happy and scary moment, as the inner realisation hit me. I was a husband, a father and had a brand-new company not making money.

The next few years were spent working all over the country promoting and selling my matches, sleeping in my car on many nights, as I scraped together enough money to pay the bills.

My son was born in March 1994. By the end of the same year, Tau Matches had gained almost 65 per cent of the match market in Botswana and needed to expand across the borders. In 1995, I successfully negotiated the house brand matches contract for a large buying group in South Africa which had more than 700 retail shops and wholesale outlets across the region. This increased Tau Matches' turnover by over 600 per cent and put me in front of my competitor, who had previously been the monopoly in South Africa.

I then opened an agency in South Africa, called Africa FMCG, to represent the match business in that country.

Sadly, through bad debt, the business lost a lot of money and we closed it down. This cost me personally most of my accrued wealth and I left Botswana and relocated to Nelspruit in South Africa to start again. This move knocked my confidence as I had been sailing the crest of the wave and was now back in the storm of survival.

I opened my next business, On Your Toes Garden and Landscaping. Over the next two years. I grew the business with a mix of large-scale projects, such as hotels, gardens, rugby fields, parks and servicing many domestic swimming pools. I serviced over 600 domestic properties with four vans and had a staff of 20. The business was growing steadily but I still felt empty and was struggling with my own inner consciousness.

In November 1997, I remember driving down the road feeling suicidal and frustrated with life and the meaning of what my life had become. I had been a leader of industry, negotiating at the highest level with multinationals and now I was cutting people's grass and cleaning their swimming pools; not where I thought I would have been.

I drove past a church and felt guided to enter the church, as I reflected on my younger years growing up, when I attended church every Sunday with my parents.

It was during this time and the subsequent months, that I felt a strong urge to follow Jesus Christ. I sold my landscaping business to a friend as I believed I had been called to do God's work.

I followed the path set in front of me and studied to become a pastor in the church. I did numerous outreach programs in Mozambique and implemented a religious film, *The Jesus Film*, as a medium to convert and bring people to the way of the Lord.

The ethos behind the church is simple.

At its heart is the conviction that everyone can know and experience the love of God for herself or himself. God's love changes us to be more Christ-like.

This led me to start my own self-funded mission called 'Servants of God' where I applied my mission work throughout the area.

The reason behind this was simple. There were structural rules and logic within the church that I did not entirely agree with. They were outside of my understanding and interpretation of the scriptures, so I felt obligated to make the change to follow a calling from God.

This was one of the most rewarding periods of my life and even though we did not have much money and relied on others to fund and supply our needs, the work was extremely fulfilling, and being guided by God I felt at peace.

The ways of the Lord are not always easy, and I believe the devil plays a huge hand in what happens when you are fully devoted to extending God's teachings.

In 2000, I had a disagreement with my then wife, and she demanded a divorce. I pleaded with her to not go ahead, however between her and her family, the decision had been made.

I had built a strong bond with my son Corbin during a time when the world seemed uncertain and the weight of the unknown pressed heavily upon us both. I found solace in the unbreakable bond I forged with my son. It was a bond built on strength and honesty, a bond that has stood the test of time, and a bond that has carried us through countless obstacles along our shared journey. As a father, I felt an unwavering sense of responsibility to guide my son through life's challenges. Little did I know that in doing so, he himself found his own logic. He learnt how to control his subconscious logic. He faced many unimaginable hurdles along the way and has stretched his logic.

As a young man seeking his place in the world, his encounters sometimes tested his resolve. He shattered the barriers that threatened to confine him, proving that strength comes not from an absence of obstacles, but from the unwavering determination to overcome them and control logic.

At that point back in my life and within myself, I was filled with grief and wanted to ensure my son, who was six years old, would be looked after. I left behind all my worldly goods, including property, furniture and whatever money was in the bank. I was put on the street with all but four garbage bags of clothing.

I slept outside in the church memorial wall area, trying to find the logic in what had happened. I went to the pastor and asked him for help, only to be told that the church does not support divorce and would not support my mission work as a divorced man. I was destroyed as both a man and father.

I went to the psychiatric hospital where I spent six weeks recovering. I was fighting my own logic and how this had happened to me. I was devastated. Could it be that I was just supposed to follow other people's logic? Had I been wrong in assuming I could change my destiny by changing logic? This had not worked out the way I had planned. It was during these six weeks of recounting my life, when I realised that failure was all part of my journey.

I moved back to my mother's home where her love and warmth gave me the strength I needed.

Early in 2001, I was off again with a new challenge to my logic. I had been searching for employment anywhere I could but to no avail.

I had an unexpected but extremely rewarding opportunity to go to the Cayman Islands, to support a company with designing, installing and commissioning the air conditioning systems for the Ritz Carlton Hotel. It was a multi-million-dollar project and I was also involved in many other smaller projects during my tenure on the island. This period strengthened my resolve and allowed me once again to look inward and question the logic in my life.

By mid-2003, I had planned on opening my own business on the Cayman Islands, but my brother wanted me to come back to Africa. I discussed this with my son who was then nine years old, and he really wanted me closer to him too. So, I accepted the opportunity and moved back to Africa.

I returned to Botswana and purchased a share of Warehousing Services Botswana which was part of the Kalahari Sales group that my brother and father still owned. This distribution business grew from strength to strength. I was working 18-hour days, with over 200 trucks, servicing over 300 shops every week. The days were long and exhausting. The essence of my logic in getting the job done became evident as the business grew.

In 2004, I met my superpower, my wife Orla. Orla's strength was not only found in her unwavering support, but also in her unwavering belief in my abilities. She saw potential in me that I didn't always recognise in myself. Her faith in my logic and decision-making abilities pushed me to strive for greatness.

Together, we embarked on a journey that defied expectations and surpassed limits. We charted new territories, both personally and professionally, always pushing forward, never settling for mediocrity. Orla's presence in my life was a constant reminder that anything is possible when you have the right person beside you.

I stand here today, proud of the path we have carved together. Orla's influence has shaped me into the strong individual I am now. Her unwavering support and steadfastness have moulded me into someone who can face any challenge head-on, unafraid, and unyielding.

As I reflect on our journey, I am filled with gratitude for Orla, my superpower. She has been the driving force behind our success, the foundation upon which our love and achievements are built. With her by my side, I know that I can conquer anything that lies ahead.

And so, I continue to sail forward, fuelled by the strength and love of my incredible wife. Together, we are an unstoppable force, a testament to the power of partnership and the beauty of unwavering support. Our love story is one of determination, resilience, and unwavering belief in one another.

With Orla as my first mate, I know that the future holds endless possibilities. Together, we will continue to sail through life's adventures, forever grateful for the day our paths intertwined, and our superpowers merged into one.

In 2006, the Kalahari Sales Group, including Warehousing Services, was sold to one of Africa's largest equity companies.

The following year, I joined Expo Botswana which had been operating since 1999 under the guidance of founder and visionary Orla McConnon, who in 2006 became Mrs Orla Bakeberg.

We grew a business on a simple motto, 'Never say no' and 'You are only as good as the last job you do'.

Expo Botswana grew quickly after that and by 2008 we started our African domination drive. First up was Expo Namibia and we were fully operational in that country, within weeks.

Namibia came about as we sat in a meeting at one of our supplier's head office, after doing work for them in Botswana. We were asked, "Can you do work in Namibia?" The answer was simple, "YES."

Neither Orla nor I had been to Namibia for work, so after the meeting, we drove from their offices in Johannesburg, to Windhoek in Namibia. There, we registered a company, found office premises, hired staff and opened a bank account, all in three days.

Returning to Botswana, I trained our new Namibian employees and manager, before sending them off with company cars and resources. They started doing Nestle work just six weeks after that customer meeting.

The global recession hit in 2009 and we had no work in Botswana or Namibia for six months. During this time one of our biggest global suppliers came to us and asked us to carry out school oral hygiene training in Zambia. We were already doing this work across Botswana and Namibia.

Expo Zambia was born in 2010, quickly followed by Expo Zimbabwe and shortly after by Expo Mozambique, all in quick succession. These were all formed because we were asked if we could do work for them in these countries and we said, "YES."

Expo Africa was then operating in five African countries covering over 70 million people, across an area twice the size of Spain, Sweden, Germany, Finland, Norway, Poland and Italy put together. Altogether, our geographical landscape was more than half the size of Europe.

We represented some of the biggest multinational food companies in the world. The company was growing rapidly and fast making a name for itself.

Expo Africa Pty Ltd officially opened a regional head office, operating out of Cape Town South Africa in 2014. All Expo Africa Offices were managed and owned by Expo Africa in Mauritius.

Swaziland and Lesotho were next to join our footprint and this brought us to being registered in nine countries, employing over 2,500 people across the region, working out of 32 depots.

We had become arguably the biggest and best promotions, marketing and logistics company in Sub-Saharan Africa, managed and owned by myself and Orla.

Our holding company in Mauritius, which all the businesses were owned by, was a brilliant structure and one that again caught the attention of the same equity company that had bought Kalahari Sales.

They again approached us in 2016 ten years after they had bought Kalahari Sales and bought the entire Expo Africa Group and merged it into their operating business. A monumental, life-changing, logic-influencing deal for both Orla and I. We had created a business and grown it to a global status, recognised by some of the world's leading, most influential brands.

After the initial handover period, we left South Africa in 2018 and headed for the Emerald Isle of Ireland, where we considered ourselves both as retired. We came back to Orla's family roots. During the previous years of visiting, I had fallen in love with Ireland. From the onset, I had always wanted to move there and become an Irish citizen.

Unfortunately, our plans changed when we had a setback regarding our contract and payments from our previous business and we were left needing a new plan. Needing to influence the logic and create an income for our lifestyle.

We then opened a three-story restaurant in Dublin. This was challenging and we sold it in February 2020. We had so much fun, but it is an extremely hard industry.

This business cost us profoundly financially, but it was fun. After all, it is only money, when it's gone.

Covid and the pandemic arrived in March 2020, two weeks after we had sold the restaurant. If we had not sold, we would have lost substantially more and that would have crippled us, as the restaurant had already drained us financially. Any chance of enjoying retirement went out the window. Being in lockdown did not suit either of us, as we needed to fund our lifestyle, so we ventured out. We also had a desire to work with others, continue our strong business message – mastering new logic.

I had registered a consulting business before we arrived in Ireland and it was time to energise this business.

I secured a contract with a courier company in Dublin that had been battling with reputation, logistics and service delivery issues. I promised them transformation, and so I worked 24 hours a day, 365 days a year, to turn it around and achieve results. I grew from general manager in Dublin to country manager, in just 18 months.

During my initial days within this business, it was often said, "A perfect peak could never be done and had never been done." (This means that every parcel is delivered before Christmas, and all their depots are empty.) Challenge accepted, and "a perfect peak" was achieved within my first 16 months. This was an incredible achievement in such a short time. My team were personally congratulated by the CEO at the highest level.

I am proud to have developed, and led, a strong team of diverse managers, leaders, couriers and staff, who all had a heart for the business, creating a culture of participation, trust and respect. We had moved the business to being victorious. Together, we achieved the unachievable.

Tripadvisor ratings moved from 2.2 to 4.7, over this time. I became the poster boy within the business, not something I ever aimed to be.

However, this achievement took every moment of my life, 24 hours a day, for 821 days, and yet was hugely self-rewarding. It took reassessing the logic of management, influencing that logic and creating a smoothly run business, to give management all that they wanted, albeit run by the logic of myself and my team. I used every ounce of my logic to change a culture and change the outcome of what is today possibly the single biggest and brightest parcel courier business in Ireland.

I believe our team's achievements were instrumental in them actually selling the business. I had truly hoped that at that point I might have been given the option to buy equity in the business, however this was not to be.

Some other managers acquired equity, including some whom I did not particularly get on with. With them all now being my bosses it became increasingly more difficult for me to protect my staff and my colleagues. The logic that we had created to be a winning formula was put under pressure by the same people who had praised it the year before. And all in the name of generating profits for the new owners, with no regard for the people who made it happen.

With the loss of my father and mother in quick succession in mid-2022, I resigned. I had decided it was then time to share my life and my passion with others. I could no longer continue to fight a fight I was never going to win, whilst watching a single man potentially destroy this business.

Not long after this relationship ended, I was given a golden opportunity to buy a global online employee engagement company – An Even Better Place to Work, bp2w® (better place 2 work). The company was originally formed to address the needs of employees within organisations.

I believe this will be the end of my story, as I have found a company where my whole ethos embraces the lifestyle I have and my logic is helping people understand that logic is flexible.

Life's experiences and Orla's comment about the *picture in the picture*, have led me to realise that I had been influencing the logic my entire life, and that I needed to share this and its relevance to anyone in business.

The Logic in The Logic.

THREE

Embracing Personal Desires & Passions

To live a life that aligns with my true self, I discovered the transformative power of embracing my logic, focusing on my desires, committing myself wholeheartedly to my passions, cultivating discipline in my actions and embracing unwavering determination.

This chapter delves deep into the profound significance of following our desires and uncovering contentment through the pursuit of our passions. Throughout my challenges, I honestly feel I have never had a bad day and I have no regrets.

Within the pages of this chapter, we embark on a journey of self-discovery and personal growth. We unravel the mysteries of our innermost desires, recognising their potential to guide us towards a life that is truly authentic and meaningful.

When I was very young, around age six, my father told me millionaires were very rich people and could do anything.

Driven, as I have always been, it became important even at that young age to be a millionaire. It took me about six years to achieve this.

Obsessed with this millionaire plan, I started collecting currency. It didn't take me long to have 100,000 Italian Lire, 500,000 Mozambique Metical, along with numerous other Kwacha and other currencies. Once added up, I had a cool million across around 11 currencies. I had done it.

It was only probably worth about 50 South African Rand back then. But to me, it was still a million as a combined number.

By exploring the importance of embracing our desires, we learn how to tap into our innermost longings, and we honour them as valuable compasses. Through self-reflection and introspection, we uncover the hidden treasures buried within our hearts and souls, allowing them to shape our path toward 'realisation'. Always remember not to hurt anybody along the way.

From my own learnings, you need to decide that when you challenge the norm, you need to be conscious of the repercussions. My father also used to say, 'For every action, there is a reaction. You determine the logic, you determine the reaction.'

Delving into the transformative power of dedicating ourselves to our passions, by wholeheartedly pursuing what sets our souls on fire, we unleash a creative force that propels us toward excellence and self-actualisation. The process by which an individual reaches his or her full potential. Always remember that self-destruction is the brother of self-actualisation and they are very similar in their differences.

We then discover the undeniable joy and satisfaction that comes from dedicating ourselves to what truly inspires us and we learn how to overcome obstacles and setbacks with resilience and determination. I have been a millionaire three times in my life, retired three times and yet here I am, still hard at it but doing what I love. Logic prescribes that I have lost millions a minimum of twice. It has been three times.

My story shares that logic is a learning. If you follow the logic of the sheep that is what you will be, a sheep. If you create your own logic, you will be faced with many trials and tribulations, many wins and many losses. Through this all, you will never be just another human living his life, until it ends.

I never wanted to, nor will I ever, arrive in heaven in showroom condition. I want to have stretched the boundaries of life and logic and I want to die with a story, even if I am the only one who reads it. I do not want to be, nor will I ever be average, rich or poor. I want to have lived uniquely.

I believe starting again, doing what you are passionate about, is what makes you happy and the people around you. Yes, my passion for being a millionaire started young but not at the cost of my happiness.

In addition, I emphasise the importance of discipline in our actions. We understand that success and fulfilment require consistent effort and commitment. Through cultivating discipline, we develop the focus and perseverance necessary to turn our desires and passions into tangible achievements.

I have a passion for motor cars. At one point in my life, I had 32 motor cars in seven years, and I lost thousands in the process. Cars are my Achilles heel, my single biggest weakness, something that I am constantly fighting.

By exploring practical strategies and techniques to enhance my discipline, I have been able to stay true to my purpose, even in the face of challenges.

The essence of unwavering determination is a journey, not a destination. I recognise that the journey towards embracing our desires and pursuing our passions is not always smooth sailing. It requires us to navigate through uncertainties, doubts and external pressures, which includes failures along the way. However, by nurturing a steadfast resolve, we can overcome these obstacles and continue our path towards self-fulfilment.

By embracing my desires, dedicating myself to my passions, exercising discipline in my actions and maintaining unwavering determination, I have unlocked the door to a life filled with purpose, joy and contentment.

So, let's continue on our voyage and unleash the power of our desires and passions, for within them lies the key to a life lived authentically and passionately.

FOUR

Cultivating a Positive Support System & Overcoming Negativity

On my journey along an unconventional path, I faced moments of isolation and I also encountered negativity from those who doubted my choices.

I was first married at 25 and my wife was only 18, our logic was never really aligned. I spent 10 years trying to be a provider and driving myself to supply her every need and in doing so I lost some of my own identity and logic.

It was not until our separation, 11 years later that I understood whilst I was constantly trying to please others, I had driven myself to a place of resentment in myself. At that moment, alone in the isolation of a small room in the back of a farm village, having lost all that was precious to me, I decided I would never again be dictated to by my own emotions. I would never again let the decisions I made or the logic I followed ever hurt me again. For it is only ourselves we must blame in these moments.

Among these challenges, I discovered a powerful tool - the ability to filter out negativity and surround myself with a supportive network of like-minded individuals, or draw on my inner strength. It was then that I realised most of my friends did not stand by me and the world became a very lonely place.

The significance of cultivating a positive support system and highlighting the profound impact it can have on our personal growth, is a testament to a life lived.

Throughout the years, I have come across individuals who questioned my decisions, undermined my aspirations, or simply failed to understand my unique perspectives and logic. It is during these moments that I have had to consciously filter out the negativity and stay focused on my path.

By recognising that the negativity of others is often a reflection of their fears and limitations, I have developed resilience and maintained unwavering determination.

However, filtering out negativity alone is not enough. To truly thrive, we must actively seek out and surround ourselves with individuals who uplift, inspire and genuinely support us.

These like-minded souls, if you can find them, become our pillars of strength, offering encouragement, understanding and a shared sense of purpose. They become our tribe, the sailors of the ship, creating an environment that nurtures our personal growth and empowers us to reach for the stars.

I have explored the steps required to build such a support system. It includes the importance of identifying our values and aligning ourselves with individuals who share similar passions and beliefs; of paramount significance is fostering meaningful connections, both online and offline, that can provide the necessary support and guidance on our journey.

Furthermore, I have uncovered the transformative effects of surrounding myself with positive influences. By immersing ourselves in environments that encourage growth, we unlock our full potential and cultivate a mindset that thrives on possibilities rather than limitations. We learn to silence the doubts within us and replace them with the empowering voices of those who believe in our capabilities.

This is my guide for those seeking to filter out negativity and create a robust support system that propels them towards personal growth. By embracing this approach, we can overcome adversity, navigate uncharted paths and truly flourish on our journey of self-discovery.

FIVE

Overcoming Judgments & Redefining Success

In this chapter, I focus on the challenges I encountered when faced with opposition and judgments from individuals who couldn't understand or support my unconventional choices. However, amid these hurdles, I remained steadfast in my belief that the true measurement of success can only be assessed once our time on this earth has come to an end.

To judge yourself as successful while alive means the only step after that is failure, and if you are not scared of failure, you cannot be successful, because you become stagnant; and that is failure. This means that your inability to progress any further prevents you from being successful.

By questioning and challenging societal definitions of success, this chapter dives into the personal triumphs that arise from living life on our terms with our own logic. It sheds light on the incredible journey of redefining success according to our values and aspirations, rather than conforming to the expectations and judgments of others.

During my early business career in Botswana, I once approached the biggest safety match making company in Southern Africa, and asked if I could sell their matches. They respectfully declined.

I am not a person who likes refusal or letting anybody else determine my destiny, so I explained to them if they did not let me sell their matches, I would open my own match making business in Botswana.

They laughed and said go ahead.

I left that meeting and went home and sat down and started negotiations with the biggest match making business in the world.

At this time, I was 27 years old and had been running my own small agency business, United Marketing, for two years.

I registered Tau Matches. Tau is lion in Setswana, and the 19th letter of the Greek alphabet (something significant to note).

The South African company immediately took me to court, claiming I was using their registered identity and trademark on my product and also using similar coloured yellow boxes. I hadn't yet made my first matchbox but only registered the trademark and company, along with printing business cards and letterheads.

In court, it was agreed that the colours could not be contested, as nobody could guarantee any specific colour when printing these boxes. I also explained Tau is the 19th letter of the Greek alphabet. Their case was thrown out of court.

A small person's logic fighting a giant. I continued in my quest.

I again approached the biggest match factory in the world, and this time I asked for a quote for machinery. Machinery which was quoted at over three million

USD back in 1992. It was about three million more than I had.

Undeterred, I applied to Sweden Grant Fund for a loan for the equipment, knowing it would not be approved. I received a letter from them acknowledging receipt of my application and that it would be processed (these were the words I wanted to see); "We are happy to acknowledge your application has been received and it will be processed in due course."

To me this meant, *we will send over the cash as soon as possible*. Good news.

I then contacted the South African match company, again, and asked if they would sell me equipment. They declined.

As a matter of transparency, I requested that they help me look for look over the equipment that I was getting from Sweden, to see if it was all right spec-wise.

They were delighted to assist me. After all, I was a 27-year-old willing to share my plans with them.

I sent them the documents along with the letter from the bank. A week or so later, they contacted me to say they had decided they wanted to help me and would hire the machinery to me. We negotiated a while and it was eventually agreed that they would also give me all the raw materials I needed, as long as I never sold into the South African market.

Tau Matches (Pty) Ltd was founded, contracts signed and machinery on its way.

Here was the logic; I had opened a match factory and not spent a cent. They believed I could not do it, I believed I could.

The business grew from strength to strength and after two years, we had secured 65 per cent of the Botswana market. Yet, I still needed more, so I approached a national distributor in South Africa and started negotiations with them to make their bespoke house brand of matches and sell them in South Africa.

I also sold my matches into Zimbabwe, but this came at a price. The company in Sweden owned the match manufacturer in Zimbabwe and being part of the biggest match-making company in the world, I knew this would upset somebody.

And it did. They made contact and were interested in negotiations, so was I.

They believed in *their* logic: 'I must be able to make matches cheaper than them.'

My logic was if I added up all I was selling and I was making a profit, that's all I needed to influence their logic.

To increase value, I signed the previously mentioned deal with the distributor in South Africa, knowing I couldn't supply.

I then flew to London to the Swedish holding company's offices and negotiated a favourable sale of my business to them. It was based on my market share in Botswana and the contract to supply the distributor in South Africa.

They would supply the company with all the equipment needed for the factory, so I could cancel with the South African company, return their machinery and continue business as usual. They agreed also in the interim to supply me with the finished product from Zimbabwe, so I could fulfil the contract I had signed with the newly signed distributor in South Africa.

The deal was signed, and I officially became a millionaire before my 35th birthday.

Let us track the logic here –

1. I influenced the logic by making the South African company believe I was immature and reckless.

2. I then influenced their logic to believe that I was going ahead and in the process of securing the funds required.

3. I influenced the logic by making the distributor believe I had the capacity to supply.

4. I influenced the biggest match company in the world into thinking that I could make matches and sell them cheaper than they could and I would take their market.

5. Finally, I influenced their logic to the extent that they believed that they could buy my business on the strength of contracts. They believed it would secure their entry into the South African market, the only other region that they had never owned and had tried to buy, but until then had not.

They did buy the business and I stayed on to ensure the contract was fulfilled and the business was profitable. **Remember logic is considered socially acceptable, fair and sensible.**

I share my experiences of overcoming the naysayers and defying the norms, showing readers the immense power and liberation that comes from embracing our true selves and creating our logic. This chapter serves as a guide to how to break free from the restraints of societal standards and pursue a more fulfilling and authentic path to success.

I have explored the uncharted territories of logic, individuality, resilience and contentment, while also inspiring myself to rise above judgments and redefine my unique versions of success.

I have been judged by many, from schoolteachers to business acquaintances, by my parents, my brothers and many others along the way.

I have been told that I will amount to nothing; I have been told to conform and live a mediocre, safe life. All this time I have reasoned with myself, to drive my logic to the end.

SIX

The Power of Individual Logic

In a world where logic is often imposed upon us, dictating our actions and confining our possibilities, it becomes crucial to question its origins and limitations. I will delve into a profound exploration of logic, urging readers to embrace their unique brand of reasoning and boldly challenge the boundaries set by others.

I completed senior school and was speedily taken in by the South African Defence Force. Conscription back then was two years. This was not something I wanted to do but realised I had no choice so I decided to make the best of the two years.

I quickly realised that officers were treated a lot better, I embarked on a plan to achieve this status. My plan was to stay off the radar as much as possible, only be seen by the officers, do many favours focusing on their needs and make sure they liked me without others knowing.

I also became a vegetarian, which meant I couldn't eat among the regular soldiers and had to eat in the officer's mess, as it was their chef who would make me vegetarian food. This worked very well as I got to know them all and when the time for selection came, I was first on their list, job done. I sat a few exams and passed which helped me for the first six months. With only 18 months left to finish my recruitment, I decided I would focus my attention on signals. I had been advised that I was to spend time on the country border of South West Africa (Namibia today), where the war was taking place between South West Africa and Angola.

I was once again not happy with this, but having control of the only way our barracks could communicate with the outside world handed me all the power to influence the logic and to influence the outcome.

Over the next 18 months, I spent more time away from the border than I did on the border. As the signals officer, I was aware of every seminar conference and training camp that was going on back home, so I enrolled in them all. Once approved, I would take it to the commanding officer and state that I had been granted a place in the current training course which led to me being sent back to South Africa.

By delving into the depths of my logic, I began to unravel the intricacies of this formation. As we question where our logic truly stems from, we gain a deeper understanding of the influences that have shaped our lives. Through this introspection, I was encouraged to recognise the immense power this held within me, to chart my path and to break free from the limits of conventional thinking.

I remember in junior school, just before my last year, when the teachers were selecting prefects. I quickly realised that being a prefect gave you some privileges that others did not have. I was under no illusion that as much as the teachers liked me, I was not going to become a prefect. This was chosen by the logic of others, as in the teachers and their logic, which didn't always align with mine.

So, I influenced their logic. I went to the library, studied and wrote an exam to be a library prefect, which I passed with flying colours and I became a library prefect.

Influence the logic, Influence the outcome.

As a library prefect I was entitled to all the privileges of a school prefect including extra benefits, which I discovered afterward.

The school heads had devised a logic for the criteria of their decision selecting prefects.

They never thought about the error in the plan. Library prefects are not chosen, they are granted this position based on performance and sitting an exam.

The limitations that logic imposes on us are often subtle and insidious. They can restrict our dreams, dampen our ambitions, and hinder our personal growth. However, by embracing our unique logic, we create a space for innovation and progress. We are inspired to challenge the status quo, to question the established norms and to push the boundaries that confine their potential.

My mom once told me if I saved ZAR100 (one hundred South African Rand), she would match it, all because she wanted me to save 100 in my savings account.

Her logic was perfect. If I saved 10 per week, over time I would have 100. This would have created a habit of saving and hopefully a habit that I might continue to have for the rest of my life.

My logic, however, was selling all you have to get 100 into the bank and then get another 100 from my mom. Buy my items back and have 100 in my hand to spend on other items.

Her logic was to create a saving habit but mine was to get the cash based on performance.

Through thought-provoking anecdotes, compelling research and insightful analysis, this chapter empowers you to trust your intuition, embrace your idiosyncrasies, and unleash the true power of your logic. By doing so, you can break free from the limitations imposed by others and forge your remarkable path in life based on performance and logic.

Interesting fact – We identify that logic and logistics are based on the same word. Both logic and logistics ultimately derive from the Greek *logos*, meaning 'reason'.

But while logic derives directly from Greek, logistics took a longer route, first passing into French as *logistique*, meaning 'art of calculating' and then into English from there.

How are logistics and logic related? Logic, used strictly in the singular, is a science that deals with the formal principles of reason. By now, you know some of my thoughts on that concept.

Generally, if a visitor walks into the house with an umbrella, it is logical for one to assume that it is raining outside.

In Africa, people use umbrellas to protect them from the heat and sun.

So, the above logic is flawed.

Logistics, which involves such processes as the delivery of personnel or supplies in an efficient manner, can often employ logic, by reasoning out the path least likely to interrupt the flow of a delivery. This logic is only perceived as reasonable.

If we continue the thought of influencing the logic, it stands to reason that a direct result would be to influence the culture.

All cultures require logistics because nothing operates without it.

In doing so, we need to form the ideal team.

This is achieved once you have influenced the logic.

The power of individual logic invites you to embark on a liberating exploration of your reasoning abilities. It allows you to challenge the authority of external influences, embrace your unique perspectives and navigate the world with confidence and authenticity.

In the end, it is through embracing and harnessing our logic that we truly discover our potential and create the life we envision.

SEVEN

The Three Steps of My Storm

Embarking on my journey towards personal satisfaction and pushing the limits of reason, required navigating through three transformative steps – The Launch, The Storm and The Landing.

In this chapter, I delve into each of these pivotal stages, unravelling the profound lessons I learned along the way.

Logic is created in your daily activity by the people around you. The only true thing about logic is its ability to be misinterpreted, misplaced, and manipulated. Not so solid now, is it?

The most dominant concept of logic is rationality. This is often confused with fact.

However, fact and rationality are different things and it is important in logical reasoning to distinguish the differences.

Rationality has to do with a logical idea rather than the fact of the idea. For example, the logic can have factual inference but an invalid rationale.

Logic, however, can also be rational but with false or untrue conclusions.

So, what does this mean?

Examples of logical reasoning are –

All rabbits are fish
All salmon are rabbits
Therefore, all salmon are fish

Logic is about how you interpret the rational and the fact behind the logic.

As mentioned, logic is defined as –

A socially acceptable, fair, and sensible or reasonable way of thinking about something.

Don't let another person's logic determine your destiny. People who follow logic remain mediocre.

People who Influence the logic stand out. We were not brought into this world to be mediocre.

Standout and be brilliant.

I use business as an example, as I am very familiar with it.

As an executive manager, I have talked with hundreds of managers over the years and can tell you that most of those executives have agreed on one thing - it is a very solitary position.

Why? For starters, everyone from board members and the executive team to employees and customers, view the executive manager as the ultimate go-to decision-maker in a company, the one who guides the logic.

The captain of the ship, or, as my colleagues used to call me, the glue that keeps it all together.

It is a unique position to hold in a company and the pressure increases as a company continues to scale.

Being able to share the logic and guide the logic becomes harder as business gets bigger.

Throughout that process, the company typically continues to differentiate its products, as well as the methodologies and processes it uses for product, customer and company development. The biggest problem is that nobody changes the logic as the company grows and they are unwavering in previous logic that is no longer relative to the full picture of the business.

This is because executives lose touch with what's happening on the ground and when this happens, the culture of the business changes negatively and so does the outcome.

And guess who's largely responsible for dealing with and overseeing all those things? The executive manager.

In short, the success or failure of a growing company ultimately lies squarely on an executive manager's shoulders. But also, their success is reliant on their teams' performance.

The executive manager is the leader - the one person expected to establish the kind of logical vision, culture and purpose that breeds high-level performance, driven by culture and the ability to change outcomes.

The bottom line is that the expansion stage is a difficult time in a company's development.

The executive manager may put on a confident face to their board, employees and customers, but the reality is it's a solitary place.

They may even come across as superheroes. But on the inside, these executives often feel a sense of loneliness, as they feel the logic and ethos of the business is forever changing. Most of the time they are required to put difficulties and distractions out of their mind, so they can focus on achieving their most important short-term goals, logically.

If you understand the logic, you can Influence the logic.

This book has three defined sections as mentioned, and yet, all are interconnected, which I will try to share with you through my life story and the ways we can all –

Influence the logic;
Personally aspire to greatness;

Influence the culture;
Allow others to understand that they too can reach greatness;

Influence the outcome;
Change the environment around you to reach greatness for all.

I have been doing this all my life without realising.

Recently as previously mentioned, I had a 'light bulb moment' that brought me to the realisation that my entire life I have been influencing the logic and working the system with results.

Influencing logic is not just the beginning of every day and every moment, but a constant process.

The human brain depends on logic to make decisions. Your logic remembers what we say and is considered socially acceptable, fair and sensible.

Just like your daily routine in your work environment, your colleagues, your bosses and their bosses, all use logic to make plans, instruct people and drive business. Why do we rely on their logic? You have your own logic. The same applies to your personal life.

Influence the logic and you can control the outcome. It is about attitude, beliefs and consequences.

Step 1: The Launch

Every great adventure begins with a leap of faith, a daring decision to venture into the unknown. That one moment in your life when you decide, to decide for yourself.

The Launch represents that exhilarating moment when I summoned the courage to break free from the constraints of convention and set sail towards uncharted territories. It was during this phase that I discovered the power of embracing uncertainty and embracing the unexpected. Accepting that things were going to go wrong - and they did, as I explained - but sometimes they worked out just like I intended. Each step forward became a testament to my strength and resilience, propelling me closer to my true purpose. Influencing my logic along the way.

Step 2: The Storm

During any transformative journey lies a tempest of challenges, trials and tribulations. The Storm represents that tumultuous period where I faced the fiercest winds and relentless waves of major corporations not accepting what I wanted to do because their logic did not relate to my plan. It was a time of self-reflection, where I confronted my deepest fears and navigated through the darkest corners of my soul. These very corners included opening over 20 businesses in over 10 countries, restarting my life numerous times, influencing my logic constantly and driving through the Storm.

Through the Storm, I learned valuable lessons in perseverance, adaptability and in the unwavering belief in my abilities and the logic I cherished. It was during these turbulent moments that I discovered my true potential for growth and resilience.

Step 3: The Landing

After conquering the treacherous storm, I arrived at the Landing - the culmination of my journey towards personal fulfilment. This phase was marked by a sense of clarity, purpose and deep self-awareness. As I stepped onto solid ground, I experienced the profound joy of realising my full potential and embracing the person I had become. This took 40 years altogether, being a captain of industry, a seasoned entrepreneur and most importantly, acknowledging and owning my failures along the way.

The Landing taught me the importance of celebrating achievements, acknowledging growth and appreciating the transformative power of the journey itself.

Through the exploration of each step of the journey, numerous business ventures and often many working in tandem, there were also many tears and negativity along the way. I had realised that upon Landing, I was meant to share my journey with others.

The Launch, the Storm, and the Landing - I invite you to begin this extraordinary odyssey toward personal fulfilment. You will unravel the profound lessons learned, inspiring you to embark on your journey of self-discovery and empowerment.

EIGHT

The Power to Shape Our Lives

Logic, the cornerstone of our decision-making process is not a rigid science with guaranteed outcomes. It is more a dynamic force, moulded by the consensus of the people who surround us. In this chapter, I reach into the profound significance of comprehending, and, more importantly, influencing the logic that ultimately shapes the course of our lives.

In 2004, I met my wife Orla on a blind date. I had been single for almost four years and had been living my logic to the fullest. I had decided never again would I choose my partner, but my partner would choose me.

We met for a blind date dinner which lasted seven hours; we spoke about our past, our present and our future. It was at that moment that I realised that I had met a like-minded lady, who shared the same passion for life that I had. Somebody else who had influenced her own logic, conquered her storm and set herself free from the constraints of societal logic. She had been driven by her logic and shaped her own life. Probably not as destructive as some of mine.

We have never influenced one another's logic and we built a multinational business together, allowing one another to set our logic free and go forward on our life of discovery.

Each day we are confronted by a multitude of choices and challenges. Our ability to reason, to analyse and to make sound judgments determines our path forward. However, it is crucial to recognise that the logic we employ is not solely our creation. It is a product of the collective mindset, the shared beliefs and the societal norms that envelope us.

The shape of our lives can be a culmination of many experiences lived or shared with others.

This is our logic; we need to stand up and embrace that; we are in control of our logic.

By unravelling the underlying mechanisms of this communal logic, we gain a profound insight into the forces that shape our thoughts, actions and aspirations.

We become equipped with the tools to question established logic and paradigms, challenge conventional wisdom and forge our unique paths.

'Metcalfe's law' says that every time you add a person to a network, the number of connections increases proportionally to the square of the number of users.

Using the same law on logic - every time you add a person to a logic, the logic increases proportionally. As a direct result, logic is not a science. There is no guarantee in logic, or its outcome. The more you structure the logic, the less plausible it will be, based on being fair and sensible. It caters only to control the masses.

If we use a business for example. The logic is written by the executive body –

3 Executives, 3 lines of Logic

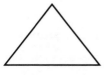

4 Executives, 6 lines of Logic

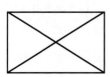

Let us generalise that –
5 Executives 10 lines of Logic
7 Executives 21 lines of Logic
9 Executives 36 lines of Logic

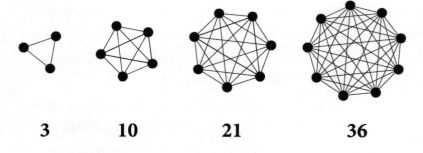

3   **10**   **21**   **36**

I love this graphic, and I think it illustrates a compelling point. The question that it poses, in my view, is how do organisations, particularly those large and/or growing, take this into account given their size and/or growth? Certainly, there is no easy answer!

If every new person added has a different temperament, interest, competency, preference and attitude, imagine how much more unstable the logic becomes.

Also, in a team, things are in a state of change and don't stay the same, lines between members will disappear and reappear due to conflicts of interest or relationships not adding value to the logic. We are complex creatures but that doesn't mean we are suited to a complex system of complex logic.

Small teams are subjects of a stable structure, and the logic is efficient.

Inefficient logic is when a player gets injured at a 5-a-side football game. That team struggles far more, than if a player gets injured at an 11-a-side game.

Everything you do will be judged by logic.

Logic is defined as - *A proper or reasonable way of thinking about something.*

Don't let others' logic determine your destiny!

People who follow others' logic remain mediocre.

People who Influence the logic stand out. Yet, understanding this is only the first step. Armed with this newfound knowledge, we have the potential to become agents of change, actively shaping the logic that governs our lives and the lives of those around us. By influencing the collective consciousness, we can challenge prevailing narratives, break down barriers and pave the way for new possibilities.

The Landing

I invite you to embark on a journey of self-discovery and empowerment. This chapter relates to business and my logic. Through thought-provoking anecdotes, we can explore how to harness the power of logic to drive positive change, both in our personal lives and in the wider world.

In my happy place in 2022, I bought a business called, An Even Better Place to Work (bp2w®). I have mentioned this previously. A global business with a head office in London, which I quickly relocated to a small village in County Mayo, Ireland. Where my wife and I had found the perfect house.

bp2w® is a global online transformational employee engagement business. I had been made aware of this business eight years previously. Using logic, it should have been run from the towers of industry, but this would have changed the course of my ship.

My logic was to create my tower of industry, my home, my castle. I quickly realised the potential I had, as somebody who has influenced logic my entire life, to make a meaningful change within businesses and influence the logic, culture and the outcome.

Business logic is created by top management based on performance and results. Can their logic be wrong? Admitting mistakes or errors is a crucial aspect of the logical process as it fosters accountability and, ultimately, progress. Several renowned scientists serve as examples of this principle.

Albert Einstein - Despite his groundbreaking work in physics, Einstein acknowledged errors in his logic. For instance, he initially included a "cosmological constant" in his theory of general relativity to explain the apparent stability of the universe, but later admitted this was a mistake.

Rosalind Franklin - Known for her work on X-ray crystallography, which contributed to our understanding the structure of DNA. Franklin also recognised a mistake in her logic when interpreting data that initially led her to believe DNA had a different structure than later confirmed.

James Watson and Francis Crick - Credited with the discovery of the structure of DNA. Watson and Crick also made mistakes. For example, their initial logic proposed a triple-stranded model for the structure of DNA that was later disproven.

In essence, admitting mistakes or errors is an essential part of the logical process, and even the most renowned scientists have made mistakes at some point in their careers. The key is to acknowledge and learn from these mistakes in order to improve logical understanding and progress.

We need to remember that thought-provoking narratives can effectively influence logic by challenging assumptions, providing practical tools and deepening understanding.

Let us unravel the intricate web of logic that binds us, empowering ourselves to become the architects of our destinies. Now is the time to embrace the influence we wield and shape a future that aligns with our deepest convictions and aspirations.

We need to strive to be visionaries. Influencing the logic, accepting our failures and embracing our successes. It is essential to be in the right place to excel.

I have found new meaning in influencing logical culture outcomes and driving logical change in business.

Influencing the culture around us:

Cultural growth finds its roots firmly planted in the ability to continually improve one's own content. This will allow one to have creative initiatives and innovations that will ensure best practices. This will develop a culture of continuous improvement in line with building a strong and resilient team that can jointly stand up and drive the business growth.

Influence the outcome:

Happiness is not about getting all you want; it is about enjoying all you have. There is always something to be thankful for.

By influencing the logic and the culture around you, you can address your outcome.

Once we fully understand the lack of real logic and can work with it, we are armed with the ability to influence logic in a manner that is not prescriptive.

Anything prescriptive involves telling people what to do. People are prescriptive when they are sure of what is right.

'You have several options' is not prescriptive,

'You should do this' is very prescriptive.

Back to the logic case study; logic should be considered socially acceptable, fair and sensible for everybody. If this is not achieved, you become prescriptive. We have discussed logic in detail. We have discussed the formulas to engage. Influencing the outcome is to fully understand each person's strategic intent.

My life has been driven by my strategic intent to influence logic and drive to greatness.

This is how it works:

Humans are historically collaborators; we have evolved that way, understanding we can accomplish more by cooperating face to face with others in a group. That's where group logic originates.

Modern organisations with their generic workstations, workplaces and increased digitised operations, foster separation and anonymity which result in a prescriptive environment.

Perceptive leaders, people who influence logic, find ways to establish deeper connections between workers. You need to allow employees the freedom to make decisions and give them the tools to assist them individually on their trajectory.

Helping employees understand the impact of what they do in their roles does not have to be complicated or expensive, it should be personalised and independently directed, allowing freedom of logic.

Employees want to know their work is noticed and valued. Making work more meaningful when people know that their actions are noticed and appreciated increases productivity and you have also influenced the outcome.

Understanding the mood in a business helps you understand the logic of teams. The teams are driven by their own set of rules and team members have their logic.

It is paramount that we create an atmosphere where everybody can influence the logic. The idea that employees work better when they feel connected is a reality. They have a common logic.

How do we do all this?

Well, first you need to know the strategic intent of each of your team members on a personal level, not only a business level, and what they want from their employment.

Strategic intent is defined by Wikipedia as –

Strategic intent can provide a sense of direction, a particular point of view about the long-term market or competitive position the organisation hopes to develop and occupy.

So, if we change organisations to employees and re-write the above definition, this is what it would read –

Strategic intent can provide a sense of direction, a particular point of view about the long-term needs of an employee, their hopes and what they want to develop and occupy.

So fundamentally, the strategic intent of your employees would mean, building a Better Place 2 Work (bp2w®).

How is that for logic?

All business development and logic should be focused on taking your employees along on the journey.

Therefore, we must understand what drives our employees and how we can work with them to provide them with their strategic intent.

It could be school fees, a new car, a holiday and so on. Whatever it is, just as you want from them you need to understand what they want from you and in doing so you work with them to get what they want.

Over time they will be actively more productive for you without even trying.

I have mentioned your employees do have the power to get you to where you need to be, so being aware of their strategic intent and sharing the company's strategic intent will benefit all involved in the end.

Let your employees have, 'The Power to Effect Change' and influence the outcome.

So, start by making your business, 'An Even Better Place 2 Work (bp2w®).'

- Influence the logic.
- Influence the culture.
- Influence the outcome.

Everything you do will be judged by logic.

Logic is defined as –

A proper or reasonable way of thinking about something

Don't let others' logic determine your destiny.

People who follow others' logic remain mediocre.

People who Influence the logic stand out.

I have lived a life full of adventures and challenges, from being a champion in ballroom and Latin American dancing to opening and managing multiple businesses across Africa, Europe and all over the world. Each experience has shaped my understanding of logic and influenced the decisions I have made.

Living in a world filled with rules and expectations, I always felt a deep sense of discomfort with the conventional path that society laid out before me. I believed that true power and uniqueness lay in the ability to shape one's own life, to create a reality that defied the limitations set by others. And so, I embarked on a journey to challenge the very fabric of logic itself.

My choices often led to isolation, but I understood that to truly live in my mind, I needed to create space for positivity and growth.

There were many moments when I faced opposition, when others disagreed with my unconventional choices. Nonetheless, I held onto a simple mantra: 'Never underestimate the ability of the less educated to manage the educated.'

I refused to let the judgments of others define my worth or success. I knew that the true measurement of my success could only come after my time on earth was done.

I proved that success and failure were not the ultimate factors of living a fulfilled life. Instead, I showed that the power of an individual's logic and the ability to mould a life according to their own beliefs and desires are the true measures of greatness.

As you read each chapter, I have wanted to inspire every person. I want you to realise that you too have the power to challenge the status quo, to live authentically and to create the life you truly want. Based on performance and your logic. I hope my journey reminds readers that the world is vast, with endless possibilities waiting to be explored.

Live life on your own terms, embrace your uniqueness, and never be afraid to challenge the boundaries of logic. For in doing so, you too can create a truly extraordinary life.

Another global entrepreneur uses the motto "Screw it just do it." My logic interprets that as "Something still must be done."

So, when others question your choices, stand firm and say, "Fuck it, I did it." Take ownership of what you do, when you do it. Ultimately, it is only upon your departure from this world that the final judgment can be made.

NINE

Embracing Simplicity – Discovering Greatness Beyond Material Things

In this final chapter, I probe into the depths of my life's experiences and reveal the constant urge I felt to change. Driven by a desire to chase the indefinable rainbow of materialistic belongings. So far, I have recounted my relentless pursuit of happiness and fulfilment through the opening and running of numerous businesses. It was through this arduous journey that I came to a profound realisation – material possessions alone and my desire for change did not hold the key. I have never had a bad day in my life, but changing direction at this stage is the most logical thing I have done.

As I reflect on my past, I have come to understand that the allure of material possessions can be deceiving. The more I acquired, the more I craved, hoping that each possession would bring me a step closer to fulfilment.

Yet, no matter how much I accumulated, the void within my soul remained unfulfilled. Influencing the logic was not a game but a journey. It was in this moment of realisation that I began to question the source of true happiness.

It was during a period of introspection that I discovered the immense power of giving back and sharing. I realised that true joy lies not in amassing wealth but in making a positive impact on other people's lives. The act of loving and caring for others became the beacon of light that guided me out of the storm of materialism.

Through my experiences, I learned that greatness is not measured by the size of your possessions or the number of businesses you own. It is that true greatness lies in the simplicity of our logic. It is in the alignment of our thoughts, actions and values that we find the essence of greatness.

I invite readers to embrace the concept of simplicity and to find their path to greatness. I underline the importance of looking beyond the allure of material things and finding fulfilment in the simplicity of life. I do not discount the value of money and material things; it is far easier to be poor and own a car than to be poor and own a bicycle, or is it? Logic must define if the car or the bicycle is more suited to your lifestyle. I am not advocating that you compromise on nice things.

It is easy for me today as I have nice things. It is during the journey that you must be aware of the logic you self-prescribe.

It is through this shift in perspective that we can discover the true meaning of logic.

A New Beginning

I have shared the profound impact that my journey has had on my life and in doing this, I offer words of wisdom and encouragement to readers who may be on their own quest for self-discovery. The storms of logic that we face can be challenging and overwhelming, but they also present an opportunity for growth and transformation.

As I embark on this new beginning, I am filled with a renewed sense of purpose and understanding. My journey has taught me that true greatness lies not in the accumulation of material possessions but in the connections we make and the love we share with others. I encourage readers to embrace their storms of logic, question societal expectations and pursue a path that aligns with their true selves.

This epilogue marks the end of my evolution but it also marks the beginning of a new chapter for myself and YOU.

It is an invitation for you to embark on your extraordinary journeys, to find the greatness that lies within yourselves and to embrace a life filled with simplicity, love and fulfilment.

If you take away one learning from this book, let it be this - 'Your logic is the driving force behind your success. Challenge logic and weather your storm.'

We are on this earth for a short time, so make it count when you are gone. Your legacy will be your legacy and your logic will remain within you; embrace it.

'Make It Fun & Get It Done'

In this book, my aim is to empower and inspire readers to break free from the constraints of the status quo and live authentically. I have delved deep into the concept of embracing personal desires, surrounding yourself with support and defying societal logic and norms. All in pursuit of creating a truly extraordinary life.

By challenging the status quo, we open ourselves up to new possibilities and opportunities. The world is constantly changing and we must adapt and evolve. Instead of adhering blindly to societal expectations and limitations, we must question the norms that restrict our growth and happiness. This book encourages readers to critically assess the rules and beliefs that govern their lives and to have the courage to make choices that align with their true desires.

Living authentically is a fundamental aspect of creating an extraordinary life. It is about being true to ourselves, embracing our unique qualities and pursuing our passions and dreams. Society often imposes pressure to conform, but by embracing our individuality we unlock our full potential. This book serves as a guide to help readers tap into their authentic selves, encouraging them to explore their passions, talents and interests and to build a life that aligns with their true identity.

Surrounding yourself with support is crucial for the journey towards an extraordinary life. Building a network of like-minded individuals who understand and encourage our aspirations can provide the necessary motivation and guidance to overcome obstacles. This book emphasises the importance of nurturing relationships with those who uplift and inspire us, and offers strategies for cultivating a strong support system. By surrounding ourselves with positive influences, we create an environment that fosters growth, resilience and success.

Defying societal logic and norms is a powerful tool for creating an extraordinary life. It requires the courage to challenge established conventions and expectations. I encourage readers to question the limitations imposed by society and to break free from the constraints that hold them back. By defying societal norms, we embrace our individuality and create a life that is truly our own.

There Is Always...
One Last Story

When I was around eight years old, my father came outside one day. There I was, with a hammer, bashing his car. My father did a backflip and shouted, "Brian, stop hitting my car with the hammer." I stopped immediately and he went off to cool down.

Moments later he came running out to see me hitting his car with a brick.

He shouted, "Brian, I told you to stop hitting my car!"

And I turned to him and said, "No Dad, you said not to hit it with a hammer."

You see the logic was there - 'Don't hit my car.' The interpretation of the situation that is socially acceptable, fair and sensible, may not be clear enough.

But the outcome was not, as the logic was overwritten by the instrument - the hammer.

If you listen carefully, you will hear the ambiguity in others' logic.

I also scratched a star onto my dad's new car once, as it was a cool car, and it deserved a star. He made it clear I was not allowed to scratch his car, mom's car or anybody's car ever, with anything. He would prefer it if I just stayed away from cars forever.

It was clear scratching was the enemy.

And loving cars is still a passion.

With Gratitude

In the vast realm of my existence, there is a force that has propelled me forward with unwavering strength and undeniable determination. It is a force that has shaped my successes, moulded my ambitions, and defined the very essence of who I am. That force is none other than my forever-loving wife, Orla. Her unwavering love and unyielding support have been the bedrock upon which I have built the foundations of my life. From the moment our paths intertwined, she has been my champion; my guiding light in a world filled with uncertainty.

Together, we have traversed the treacherous terrain of entrepreneurship, building multinational businesses that stand as testaments to our shared logic and unwavering resolve. Through the highs and lows, Orla's wisdom has been a beacon of clarity, guiding me towards capturing the true essence of my own logic.

Our journey together extends far beyond the confines of boardrooms and bottom lines. We have explored the world, venturing into the unknown with hearts full of curiosity and spirits ablaze with the desire to uncover the wonders that lie beyond our comfort zones. From the bustling streets of Johannesburg to the tranquil shores of Lake Malawi, we have shared countless adventures, painting vivid memories onto the canvas of our lives.

Laughter has become the soundtrack of our existence, filling our days with joy and our hearts with warmth.

We have forged a bond so strong, that even the fiercest of storms cannot break its unyielding grip. And in the midst of life's chaos, Orla, you remain my steady compass, helping me navigate the tumultuous sea of existence, with a strength that knows no bounds.

For it is through your boundless love and support that I have become the person I am today. You have taught me the importance of embracing my own logic, of capturing the essence of who I am and channelling it into everything I do. With you by my side, there is no limit to what we can achieve, no obstacle too great to overcome.

So, to my forever-loving wife, Orla, this book is dedicated. May its words forever serve as a testament to the strength of our love and the power of capturing the logic within our lives. Together, we have created a destiny that knows no bounds—a destiny fuelled by the unwavering strength of our hearts and the unyielding power of our love.

To my brothers, Ronald and Colin

I am forever grateful for the invaluable life lessons you have taught me. You have stood by my side during the most challenging times, being both my harshest critics and unwavering allies. Though you may not always comprehend my logic, your presence has been a constant source of strength.

Ronald, with your sharp mind and analytical thinking, you have pushed me to challenge my own thoughts and beliefs. Your critical eye has pushed me to examine every angle, forcing me to dig deeper and truly understand the world around me. Your honest feedback has been a gift, for it has allowed me to grow and learn in ways I never thought possible.

Colin, your unwavering loyalty has been my anchor in stormy seas. When I doubted myself, you were there, reminding me of my worth and encouraging me to never give up. Your unwavering support has given me the courage to face adversity head-on and push through even the toughest of challenges. You have taught me the importance of family, of standing together through thick and thin. Your bond with me has shown me the power of unity, reminding me that I am never alone in this world. And for that, I am eternally grateful.

Though there may be times when my logic seems foreign to you, I know that you will always be there, ready to listen and support me. Our differences only serve to strengthen our bond, for it is through understanding and accepting each other's perspectives that we truly grow.

Words to my son, Corbin

In the realm of life, my son, Corbin, let your eyes be the guiding light that illuminates every room you enter. May their brilliance lead others towards positivity and hope. Let your gentle character shine through, for it is through kindness and compassion that true strength is found. As you embark on the journey of life, remember this: I was not always right, at least according to some people's logic. But, my son, do not be swayed by the opinions of others. Instead, embrace your own unique logic, the one that speaks to your heart and soul. Trust in your instincts and trust in yourself, for you are capable of conquering any challenge that comes your way.

With each passing day, I eagerly await the years ahead, filled with anticipation to witness your growth and triumphs. It is with a strong determination that I know you will overcome obstacles, turning them into stepping stones towards greatness. Your unwavering spirit will be your guiding force, pushing you forward and leading you towards success.

Remember, my son, that strength does not always mean the absence of weakness. It lies in acknowledging our vulnerabilities, embracing them, and using them as fuel to rise above. In the face of adversity, may you stand tall, unwavering in your conviction to fight for what you believe in.

May your path be filled with joy and fulfilment, and may you always find solace in the pursuit of your passions. As you navigate through the complexities of the world, never forget the power of love and empathy. Extend a helping hand to those in need, for it is in giving that we receive the greatest rewards.

My son, Corbin, the world awaits your presence; stand tall and respect yourself. May your strong spirit and unwavering determination be the driving forces that propel you towards greatness. Embrace every challenge as an opportunity for growth, and may your journey be filled with triumphs that leave a lasting legacy.

In memory of my parents who both passed away in 2022

To the memory of my beloved mother, LeeLee. Throughout my childhood, she never wavered in her belief in me, as she nurtured my passion for justice and morality. She instilled in me a deep sense of compassion, respect for others, and the importance of never causing harm. I think she secretly embarrassed my logic.

My father, Big Dad, was a remarkable man, possessing a presence that could only be described as mighty. Although he didn't always understand me until later in life, he remained a steadfast supporter of our family. He was always proud of the outcomes that I shared.

In a world that often tries to dim our spirits and stifle our voices, my mother's unwavering belief in me was like a shield, protecting me from doubt and encouraging me to stand up for what is right. Her strong presence in my life moulded me into a person who strives to make a difference and champion justice.

As I grew older, I realised that my mother's belief in me was not merely blind faith, but rather a deep understanding of my potential. She saw the fire in my eyes, the burning desire to make the world a better place. And she fanned those flames, encouraging me to pursue my passion with unwavering determination.

But it wasn't just my mother who played a vital role in shaping me. My father, Big Dad, may not have always understood my logic in the moment, but he knew that I had a purpose. He stood beside me, offering his unwavering support and cheering me on. His mighty presence served as a reminder that I was never alone in my journey.

Together, my parents taught me the importance of resilience, perseverance, and staying true to my convictions. They instilled within me a sense of duty to stand up for justice and morality, no matter the challenges that lay ahead.

Today, as I reflect on the memories of my mother and father, I am filled with a deep sense of gratitude. Their belief in me, their support, and their love, have shaped me into the strong individual I am today. They may no longer be physically present, but their legacy lives on within me.

In honour of my beloved parents, I will continue to carry their teachings with me, spreading compassion, respect, and a commitment to doing what is right. They have left an indelible mark on my soul, and I am forever grateful for the strength they have bestowed upon me.

To LeeLee, my beloved mother, and Big Dad, my remarkable father, thank you for believing in me and pushing me to be the best version of myself. I will make you proud, and I will continue to champion justice and morality, just as you did. Your memory will forever be a guiding light in my journey.